Quotes And Images From Christopher Columbus

Filson Young

[ZHINGOORA BOOKS]

About Author

Alexander Bell Filson Young was a journalist, BBC programme advisor and author. His wrote the book on Titanic, a RMS Titanic ship. His famous works include: Titanic, The Relief of Mafeking and etc.

COLUMBUS

SAN SALVADOR
OR
WATLING ISLAND

A man standing on the sea-shore

Absent for a little time, and his

organisation went to pieces

All days, however hard, have an

evening, and all journeys an end

Amerigo Vespucci

And every one goes naked and
unashamed

At last extricate himself from the

theological stupor

Attempts that have been made to
glorify

him socially

Bede, in the eighth century,

established it finally (sphericity)

Began to offer bargains to the Almighty

Believed that the Spaniards came from

heaven

Biography which obscures the truth with

legends and pretences

Cannibal epicures did not care for the

flesh of women and boys

Christian era denied the theory of the

roundness of the earth

Columbus, calling for an egg, laid a

wager

Columbus never once mentions his wife

Columbus's habit of being untruthful in

regard to his own past

Cooling off in his enthusiasm as the

pastime became a task

Desire to get a great deal of money

without working for it

Diminishing object to the wet eyes of

his mother, sailed away

Dogs wagged their tails, but that never

barked

Establishment of ten footmen and twenty

other servants

Exchanging the natives for cattle

First known discovery of tobacco by

Europeans

First organised transaction of slavery

on the part of Columbus

Freed by force and with guns

Having issued three Bulls in twenty-four hours,

he desisted

He had a way of rising above petty

indignities

He was a great stickler for the

observances of religion

Hearts quick to burn, quick to forget

Heretics were being burned every year

by the Grand Inquisitor

High time, indeed, that they should be

taught to wear clothing

Idea of importing black African labour

to the New World

Ideas to him were of more value than

facts

If there were no results, there would

be no rewards

Inclined to be pompous

Irving: so inaccurate, so untrue to

life, and so profoundly dull

Islands in that sea had their greatest

length east and west

Juan Ponce de Leon, the discoverer of

Florida

Learn the blessings of Christianity

under the whip

Lives happily in our dreams, as blank

as sunshine

Logic is irresistible if you only grant

the first little step

Loose way in which the term India was

applied in the Middle Ages

Man with a Grievance

Man of single rather than manifold

ideas

More than a touch of crafty and

elaborate dissimulation

Nautical phrase "make it so."

Never to deal with subordinates

No more troubled by any wonder, sleeps

at last

No Spanish women accompanied it (2d

expedition)

Nothing so ludicrous as an Idea to

those who do not share it

Only confirmative evidence remained

Patience which holds men back from

theorising

Presence of the owner makes the horse

fat

Professors of Christ brought not peace,

but a sword

Religion has in our days fallen into

decay

Saw potatoes also, although they did

not know what they were

Sea of Darkness

Seeking to hire the protection of the

Virgin

She must either sin or be celibate

Shifts and deceits that he practised

Spaniards sometimes hanged thirteen of

them in a row

Spaniards undertook to teach the

heathen the Christian religion

St. Chrysostom opposed the theory of

the earth's roundness

Stayed till night to eat their sop for

fear of seeing (weevils)

Stuffed so full indeed that eyes and

ears are closed

Tasks that are the common heritage of

all small boys

Terror and amazement; they had never

seen horses before

The cross and the sword, the whip-lash

and the Gospel

The great thing in those days was to

discover something

The missionary walked beside the

slave-driver

The terrified seamen making vows to the

Virgin

Theologians, however, proved equal to

the occasion

There is deception and untruth somewhere

They saw the past in the light of the

present

Took himself and the world very

seriously

Vague longing and unrest that is the

life-force of the world

When the pot boils the scum rises to

the surface

Who never could meet any trouble

without grumbling

The End

www.ingramcontent.com/pod-product-compliance
Lightning Source LLC
Chambersburg PA
CBHW060023300526
45794CB00003B/1269